The What's Good?

Gratitude Journal for Kids

2022 BYC Publishing©

Want free Stuff?

Email us at:
bycpublishing@gmail.com

Write "Free Gift" on the subject line of your email and we'll send you a fun, free gift!

This book belongs to:

_____

_____

_____

Thank You!

The What's Good? Gratitude Journal for Kids

Think of the last time someone gave you a gift or did something nice for you. How did you feel? **Were you excited?** That's part of the feeling of gratitude. Another part of gratitude is feeling thankful and showing appreciation for the good things that come your way and the special people that are in your life. Gratitude is a positive emotion. It can help you feel happier. **The What's Good?** *Gratitude Journal for Kids*, helps you to focus on your days and remember the good things that happened! The journal is easy to use. Just follow the steps below to complete the pages in the journal. It only takes a few minutes to finish a page.

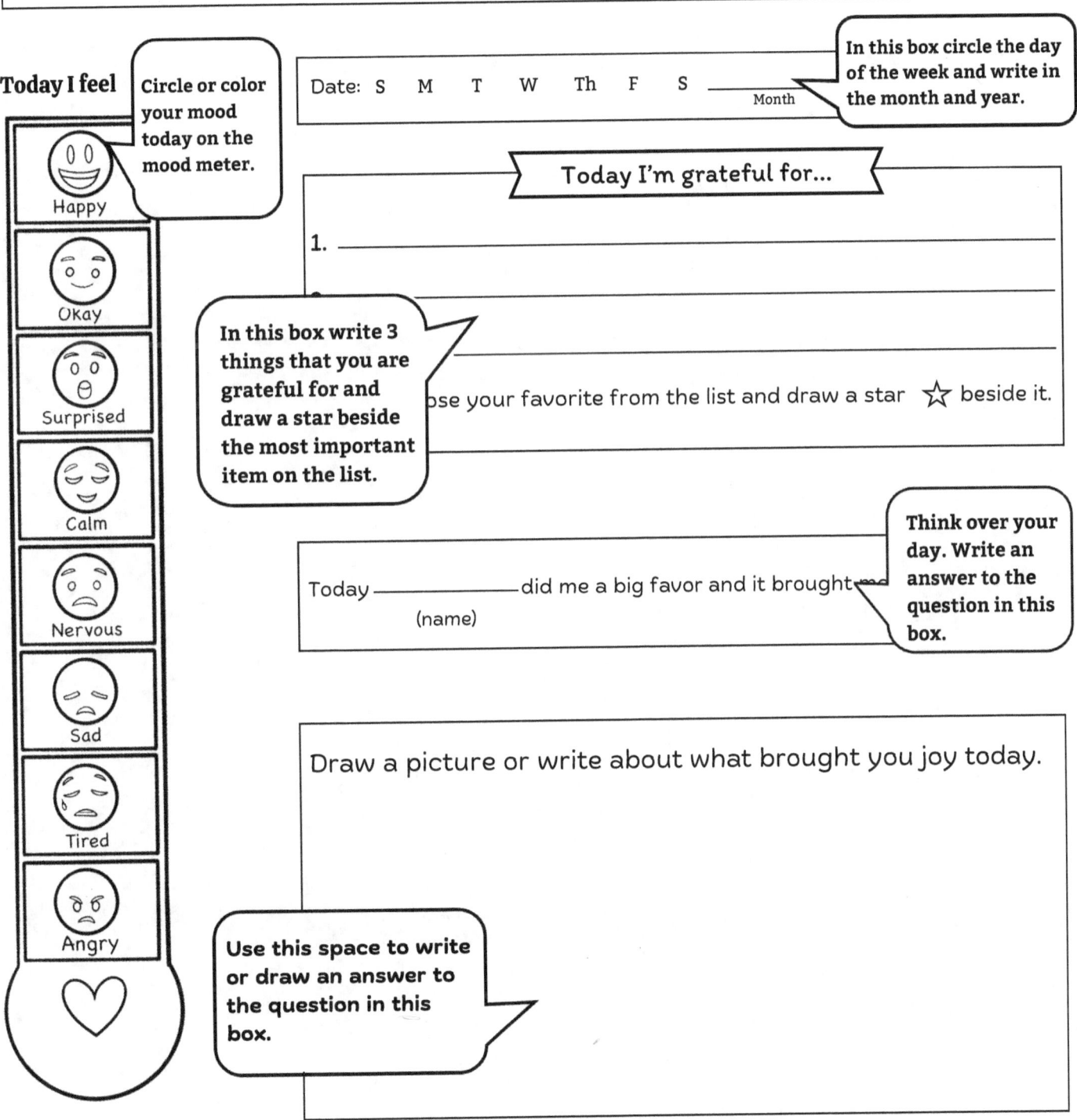

Today I feel

Circle or color your mood today on the mood meter.

Happy
Okay
Surprised
Calm
Nervous
Sad
Tired
Angry

In this box circle the day of the week and write in the month and year.

Date: S   M   T   W   Th   F   S _____
Month

Today I'm grateful for...

1. _____

In this box write 3 things that you are grateful for and draw a star beside the most important item on the list.

...ose your favorite from the list and draw a star ☆ beside it.

Today _____ did me a big favor and it brought...

(name)

Think over your day. Write an answer to the question in this box.

Draw a picture or write about what brought you joy today.

Use this space to write or draw an answer to the question in this box.

Date: S   M   T   W   Th   F   S   _____ / _____
                                              Month   Year

Today I feel

Happy

Okay

Surprised

Calm

Nervous

Sad

Tired

Angry

Today I'm grateful for...

1. _____

2. _____

3. _____

4. Choose your favorite from the list and draw a star ☆ beside it.

Today I'm most grateful because _____ brought
me joy.   (someone or something)

What is one other thing that was nice about today? Draw a
picture or write about it.

Date: S   M   T   W   Th   F   S   _____ / _____
                                          Month   Year

Today I feel

Happy

Okay

Surprised

Calm

Nervous

Sad

Tired

Angry

Today I'm grateful for...

1. _____

2. _____

3. _____

4. Choose your favorite from the list and draw a star ☆ beside it.

Today I'm most grateful because _____ brought me joy.
                                        (someone or something)

What is one other thing that was nice about today? Draw a picture or write about it.

Date: S   M   T   W   Th   F   S   _____ / _____
                                          Month   Year

Today I feel

Happy

Okay

Surprised

Calm

Nervous

Sad

Tired

Angry

Today I'm grateful for...

1. _____

2. _____

3. _____

4. Choose your favorite from the list and draw a star ☆ beside it.

Today I'm most grateful because _____ brought me joy.   (someone or something)

What is one other thing that was nice about today? Draw a picture or write about it.

Date: S   M   T   W   Th   F   S   _____ /_____
                                              Month   Year

Today I feel

- Happy
- Okay
- Surprised
- Calm
- Nervous
- Sad
- Tired
- Angry

Today I'm grateful for...

1. _____

2. _____

3. _____

4. Choose your favorite from the list and draw a star ☆ beside it.

Today I'm most grateful because _____ brought me joy.   (someone or something)

What is one other thing that was nice about today? Draw a picture or write about it.

Date: S M T W Th F S _____ / _____
                                    Month   Year

Today I feel

Happy

Okay

Surprised

Calm

Nervous

Sad

Tired

Angry

Today I'm grateful for...

1. _____

2. _____

3. _____

4. Choose your favorite from the list and draw a star ☆ beside it.

Today_____did me a big favor and it brought me joy.
        (name)

Draw a picture or write about what brought you joy today.

Date: S   M   T   W   Th   F   S   _____ / _____
                                        Month   Year

Today I feel

☺ Happy
☺ Okay
☺ Surprised
☺ Calm
☹ Nervous
☹ Sad
☹ Tired
☹ Angry
♡

Today I'm grateful for...

1. _____

2. _____

3. _____

4. Choose your favorite from the list and draw a star ☆ beside it.

One thing that I do to show others that I am grateful is_____
_____ .

Write about or draw a picture of what you do to show someone that you are grateful for something that they've done for you.

Date: S   M   T   W   Th   F   S   _____ / _____
                                                Month   Year

Today I feel

Happy

Okay

Surprised

Calm

Nervous

Sad

Tired

Angry

Today I'm grateful for...

1. _____

2. _____

3. _____

4. Choose your favorite from the list and draw a star ⭐ beside it.

Today I'm most grateful because _____ brought
me joy.   (someone or something)

What is one other thing that was nice about today? Draw a
picture or write about it.

Date: S M T W Th F S _____ / _____

Month / Year

Today I feel

- Happy
- Okay
- Surprised
- Calm
- Nervous
- Sad
- Tired
- Angry

Today I'm grateful for...

1. _____

2. _____

3. _____

4. Choose your favorite from the list and draw a star ☆ beside it.

Today I'm most grateful because _____ brought me joy.

(someone or something)

What is one other thing that was nice about today? Draw a picture or write about it.

Date: S   M   T   W   Th   F   S   _____ / _____
                                          Month   Year

Today I feel

Happy

Okay

Surprised

Calm

Nervous

Sad

Tired

Angry

Today I'm grateful for...

1. _____

2. _____

3. _____

4. Choose your favorite from the list and draw a star ☆ beside it.

Today I'm most grateful because _____ brought me joy.
                                        (someone or something)

What is one other thing that was nice about today? Draw a picture or write about it.

Date: S   M   T   W   Th   F   S   _____ / _____
                                      Month   Year

Today I feel

😁	Happy
🙂	Okay
😮	Surprised
😌	Calm
😟	Nervous
😢	Sad
😫	Tired
😠	Angry
♡	

Today I'm grateful for...

1. _____

2. _____

3. _____

4. Choose your favorite from the list and draw a star ☆ beside it.

Even on days when I'm not my happiest, I'm still grateful because

_____ .

What was your favorite thing about today? Draw a picture or write about it.

Date: S M T W Th F S _____ / _____
Month   Year

Today I feel

Happy

Okay

Surprised

Calm

Nervous

Sad

Tired

Angry

Today I'm grateful for...

1. _____

2. _____

3. _____

4. Choose your favorite from the list and draw a star ☆ beside it.

Today I'm most grateful because _____ brought
me joy.   (someone or something)

What is one other thing that was nice about today? Draw a
picture or write about it.

Date: S   M   T   W   Th   F   S   _____ / _____

Month   Year

Today I feel

Happy

Okay

Surprised

Calm

Nervous

Sad

Tired

Angry

Today I'm grateful for...

1. _____

2. _____

3. _____

4. Choose your favorite from the list and draw a star ☆ beside it.

Today I'm most grateful because _____ brought me joy.   (someone or something)

What is one other thing that was nice about today? Draw a picture or write about it.

Date: S   M   T   W   Th   F   S   _____ /_____
                                    Month   Year

Today I feel

Happy

Okay

Surprised

Calm

Nervous

Sad

Tired

Angry

Today I'm grateful for...

1. _____

2. _____

3. _____

4. Choose your favorite from the list and draw a star ☆ beside it.

Today I'm most grateful because _____ brought
me joy.   (someone or something)

What is one other thing that was nice about today? Draw a
picture or write about it.

Date: S   M   T   W   Th   F   S _____ / _____

Month   Year

Today I feel

Happy

Okay

Surprised

Calm

Nervous

Sad

Tired

Angry

Today I'm grateful for...

1. _____

2. _____

3. _____

4. Choose your favorite from the list and draw a star ⭐ beside it.

Sometimes it's good to say thank you to let others know that you are grateful for something that they have given you or done for you. Today I will say thank you to _____ .

What did you say thank you for today? Draw a picture or write about it.

Date: S M T W Th F S _____ / _____
Month / Year

Today I feel

Happy

Okay

Surprised

Calm

Nervous

Sad

Tired

Angry

Today I'm grateful for...

1. _____

2. _____

3. _____

4. Choose your favorite from the list and draw a star ☆ beside it.

Today I'm most grateful for _____

because _____ .

What is your favorite thing about today? Draw a picture or write about it.

Date: S   M   T   W   Th   F   S   _____ / _____
                                             Month   Year

Today I feel

Happy

Okay

Surprised

Calm

Nervous

Sad

Tired

Angry

Today I'm grateful for...

1. _____

2. _____

3. _____

4. Choose your favorite from the list and draw a star ☆ beside it.

My best gift ever is _____ . I am very grateful for it because _____ .

What did you do to show that you were grateful for your favorite gift? Draw a picture or write about it.

Date: S M T W Th F S _____ / _____
Month   Year

Today I feel

Happy

Okay

Surprised

Calm

Nervous

Sad

Tired

Angry

Today I'm grateful for...

1. _____

2. _____

3. _____

4. Choose your favorite from the list and draw a star ☆ beside it.

Today I'm most grateful because _____ brought me joy.   (someone or something)

What is one other thing that was nice about today? Draw a picture or write about it.

Date: S M T W Th F S _____/_____
                                    Month   Year

Today I feel

Happy

Okay

Surprised

Calm

Nervous

Sad

Tired

Angry

Today I'm grateful for...

1. _____

2. _____

3. _____

4. Choose your favorite from the list and draw a star ☆ beside it.

Today I'm most grateful because _____ brought me joy.
                                        (someone or something)

What is one other thing that was nice about today? Draw a picture or write about it.

Date: S   M   T   W   Th   F   S   _____ / _____
                                        Month   Year

Today I feel

Happy

Okay

Surprised

Calm

Nervous

Sad

Tired

Angry

Today I'm grateful for...

1. _____

2. _____

3. _____

4. Choose your favorite from the list and draw a star ⭐ beside it.

Today I'm most grateful because _____ brought
me joy.   (someone or something)

What is one other thing that was nice about today? Draw a
picture or write about it.

Date: S   M   T   W   Th   F   S   _____ / _____
                                    Month   Year

Today I feel

- Happy
- Okay
- Surprised
- Calm
- Nervous
- Sad
- Tired
- Angry

Today I'm grateful for...

1. _____

2. _____

3. _____

4. Choose your favorite from the list and draw a star ☆ beside it.

One of my favorite colors is _____.
One thing that's my favorite color that I'm grateful for is _____
_____.

Draw a picture or write about things in your favorite color that bring you joy.

Date: S M T W Th F S _____ / _____
                                    Month   Year

Today I feel

- Happy
- Okay
- Surprised
- Calm
- Nervous
- Sad
- Tired
- Angry

Today I'm grateful for...

1. _____

2. _____

3. _____

4. Choose your favorite from the list and draw a star ☆ beside it.

Today I'm most grateful because _____ brought
me joy.   (someone or something)

What is one other thing that was nice about today? Draw a
picture or write about it.

Date: S   M   T   W   Th   F   S   _____ / _____

Month   Year

Today I feel

Happy

Okay

Surprised

Calm

Nervous

Sad

Tired

Angry

Today I'm grateful for...

1. _____

2. _____

3. _____

4. Choose your favorite from the list and draw a star ☆ beside it.

Today I'm most grateful because _____ brought
me joy.   (someone or something)

What is one other thing that was nice about today? Draw a
picture or write about it.

Date: S   M   T   W   Th   F   S   _____ / _____
                                    Month   Year

Today I feel

Happy

Okay

Surprised

Calm

Nervous

Sad

Tired

Angry

Today I'm grateful for...

1. _____

2. _____

3. _____

4. Choose your favorite from the list and draw a star ☆ beside it.

Today I'm most grateful because _____ brought me joy.   (someone or something)

What is one other thing that was nice about today? Draw a picture or write about it.

Date: S M T W Th F S _____ / _____
                                        Month   Year

Today I feel

Happy

Okay

Surprised

Calm

Nervous

Sad

Tired

Angry

Today I'm grateful for...

1. _____

2. _____

3. _____

4. Choose your favorite from the list and draw a star ☆ beside it.

One of my favorite treats is _____ .

When I'm enjoying my favorite treat I _____
to show that I'm grateful for it.

Draw a picture or write about a day that you were grateful
because you had your favorite treat.

Date: S M T W Th F S _____ / _____
                                    Month   Year

Today I feel

Happy

Okay

Surprised

Calm

Nervous

Sad

Tired

Angry

Today I'm grateful for...

1. _____

2. _____

3. _____

4. Choose your favorite from the list and draw a star ☆ beside it.

My friend _____ is very good at _____ .

I'm not good at what my friend is good at but I'm very grateful for

being good at _____ .

Draw a picture or write about a skill or talent that you are grateful for.

Date: S M T W Th F S _____ / _____
Month   Year

Today I feel

Happy

Okay

Surprised

Calm

Nervous

Sad

Tired

Angry

Today I'm grateful for...

1. _____

2. _____

3. _____

4. Choose your favorite from the list and draw a star ☆ beside it.

Today I'm most grateful because _____ brought
me joy.   (someone or something)

What is one other thing that was nice about today? Draw a
picture or write about it.

Date: S   M   T   W   Th   F   S   _____ / _____
                                          Month   Year

Today I feel

| Happy |
| Okay |
| Surprised |
| Calm |
| Nervous |
| Sad |
| Tired |
| Angry |

Today I'm grateful for...

1. _____

2. _____

3. _____

4. Choose your favorite from the list and draw a star ☆ beside it.

Today I'm most grateful because _____ brought
me joy.   (someone or something)

What is one other thing that was nice about today? Draw a
picture or write about it.

Date: S   M   T   W   Th   F   S _____ / _____

Month   Year

Today I feel

Happy

Okay

Surprised

Calm

Nervous

Sad

Tired

Angry

♡

Today I'm grateful for...

1. _____

2. _____

3. _____

4. Choose your favorite from the list and draw a star ☆ beside it.

Today I'm most grateful because _____ brought me joy.   (someone or something)

What is one other thing that was nice about today? Draw a picture or write about it.

Date: S   M   T   W   Th   F   S   _____ / _____
                                              Month   Year

Today I feel

😀 Happy
🙂 Okay
😮 Surprised
😌 Calm
🙁 Nervous
😞 Sad
😫 Tired
😠 Angry
♡

Today I'm grateful for...

1. _____

2. _____

3. _____

4. Choose your favorite from the list and draw a star ☆ beside it.

One of my favorite books is _____. I'm very

grateful for it because _____ .

Draw a picture or write about one other thing about your favorite book that makes you grateful.

Date: S M T W Th F S _____ / _____
                                    Month   Year

Today I feel

Happy

Okay

Surprised

Calm

Nervous

Sad

Tired

Angry

Today I'm grateful for...

1. _____

2. _____

3. _____

4. Choose your favorite from the list and draw a star ☆ beside it.

Days won't always be perfect but even on imperfect days there is always something to be grateful for. What happened to you today that was a little imperfect?

_____

_____

Draw a picture or write about what brought you joy on an imperfect day.

Date: S   M   T   W   Th   F   S   _____ / _____
                                            Month   Year

Today I feel

- Happy
- Okay
- Surprised
- Calm
- Nervous
- Sad
- Tired
- Angry

Today I'm grateful for...

1. _____

2. _____

3. _____

4. Choose your favorite from the list and draw a star ☆ beside it.

Today I'm most grateful because _____ brought
me joy.   (someone or something)

What is one other thing that was nice about today? Draw a
picture or write about it.

Date: S   M   T   W   Th   F   S   _____ / _____

Month   Year

Today I feel

Happy

Okay

Surprised

Calm

Nervous

Sad

Tired

Angry

Today I'm grateful for...

1. _____

2. _____

3. _____

4. Choose your favorite from the list and draw a star ☆ beside it.

Today I'm most grateful because _____ brought me joy.

(someone or something)

What is one other thing that was nice about today? Draw a picture or write about it.

Date: S   M   T   W   Th   F   S   _____ / _____
                                          Month   Year

Today I feel

Happy

Okay

Surprised

Calm

Nervous

Sad

Tired

Angry

Today I'm grateful for...

1. _____

2. _____

3. _____

4. Choose your favorite from the list and draw a star ☆ beside it.

Today I'm most grateful because _____ brought
me joy.   (someone or something)

What is one other thing that was nice about today? Draw a
picture or write about it.

Date: S   M   T   W   Th   F   S   _____ / _____
                                               Month   Year

Today I feel

- Happy
- Okay
- Surprised
- Calm
- Nervous
- Sad
- Tired
- Angry

Today I'm grateful for...

1. _____

2. _____

3. _____

4. Choose your favorite from the list and draw a star ☆ beside it.

One of my favorite movies is _____ .
I'm grateful for it because _____ .

We can be grateful for people and things! Today write a note to someone that you are grateful for. Tell them why you are grateful for them.

Dear_____,

I'm grateful for you because _____

_____

_____

_____ .

Sincerely,

_____

Date: S   M   T   W   Th   F   S   _____/_____
                                    Month   Year

Today I feel

- Happy
- Okay
- Surprised
- Calm
- Nervous
- Sad
- Tired
- Angry

Today I'm grateful for...

1. _____

2. _____

3. _____

4. Choose your favorite from the list and draw a star ☆ beside it.

Today I'm most grateful because _____ brought me joy.   (someone or something)

What is one other thing that was nice about today? Draw a picture or write about it.

Date: S   M   T   W   Th   F   S   _____ / _____
                                            Month   Year

Today I feel

Happy

Okay

Surprised

Calm

Nervous

Sad

Tired

Angry

Today I'm grateful for...

1. _____

2. _____

3. _____

4. Choose your favorite from the list and draw a star ☆ beside it.

Today I'm most grateful because _____ brought me joy.
                                              (someone or something)

What is one other thing that was nice about today? Draw a picture or write about it.

Date: S M T W Th F S _____/_____
Month   Year

Today I feel

- Happy
- Okay
- Surprised
- Calm
- Nervous
- Sad
- Tired
- Angry

Today I'm grateful for...

1. _____

2. _____

3. _____

4. Choose your favorite from the list and draw a star ☆ beside it.

Today I'm most grateful because _____ brought me joy.   (someone or something)

What is one other thing that was nice about today? Draw a picture or write about it.

Date: S   M   T   W   Th   F   S   _____ / _____

Month   Year

Today I feel

Happy

Okay

Surprised

Calm

Nervous

Sad

Tired

Angry

Today I'm grateful for...

1. _____

2. _____

3. _____

4. Choose your favorite from the list and draw a star ☆ beside it.

The first day of school this year was _____ . One thing that brought me joy was _____ .

Draw a picture or write about what brought you joy today.

Date: S   M   T   W   Th   F   S   _____ / _____
                                          Month   Year

Today I feel

- Happy
- Okay
- Surprised
- Calm
- Nervous
- Sad
- Tired
- Angry

Today I'm grateful for...

1. _____

2. _____

3. _____

4. Choose your favorite from the list and draw a star ☆ beside it.

Today I'm most grateful because _____ brought me joy.
                                          (someone or something)

What is one other thing that was nice about today? Draw a picture or write about it.

Date: S   M   T   W   Th   F   S   _____ / _____
                                           Month   Year

Today I feel

- Happy
- Okay
- Surprised
- Calm
- Nervous
- Sad
- Tired
- Angry

Today I'm grateful for...

1. _____

2. _____

3. _____

4. Choose your favorite from the list and draw a star ☆ beside it.

Today I'm most grateful because _____ brought
me joy.   (someone or something)

What is one other thing that was nice about today? Draw a
picture or write about it.

Date: S   M   T   W   Th   F   S   _____ / _____
Month   Year

Today I feel

- 😀 Happy
- 🙂 Okay
- 😮 Surprised
- 😌 Calm
- 😟 Nervous
- 😔 Sad
- 😫 Tired
- 😠 Angry
- ♡

Today I'm grateful for...

1. _____

2. _____

3. _____

4. Choose your favorite from the list and draw a star ☆ beside it.

Today I'm most grateful because _____ brought
me joy.   (someone or something)

What is one other thing that was nice about today? Draw a
picture or write about it.

Date: S   M   T   W   Th   F   S   _____ / _____
                                              Month   Year

Today I feel

- Happy
- Okay
- Surprised
- Calm
- Nervous
- Sad
- Tired
- Angry

Today I'm grateful for...

1. _____

2. _____

3. _____

4. Choose your favorite from the list and draw a star ☆ beside it.

On the last day of school, the thing I'm most grateful for is _____
_____.

Draw a picture or write about how you show others what you are grateful on the last day of school.

Date: S   M   T   W   Th   F   S   _____ / _____
                                            Month   Year

Today I feel

😀 Happy
🙂 Okay
😮 Surprised
😌 Calm
🙁 Nervous
😔 Sad
😫 Tired
😠 Angry
♡

Today I'm grateful for...

1. _____

2. _____

3. _____

4. Choose your favorite from the list and draw a star ☆ beside it.

My favorite thing about myself is_____.

I am grateful for it because _____.

Draw a picture or write about what brought you joy today.

Date: S   M   T   W   Th   F   S   _____ / _____
Month   Year

Today I feel

Happy

Okay

Surprised

Calm

Nervous

Sad

Tired

Angry

Today I'm grateful for...

1. _____

2. _____

3. _____

4. Choose your favorite from the list and draw a star ☆ beside it.

Today I'm most grateful because _____ brought me joy.   (someone or something)

What is one other thing that was nice about today? Draw a picture or write about it.

Date: S M T W Th F S _____ /_____
Month   Year

Today I feel

Happy

Okay

Surprised

Calm

Nervous

Sad

Tired

Angry

Today I'm grateful for...

1. _____

2. _____

3. _____

4. Choose your favorite from the list and draw a star ☆ beside it.

Today I'm most grateful because _____ brought me joy.   (someone or something)

What is one other thing that was nice about today? Draw a picture or write about it.

Date: S   M   T   W   Th   F   S   _____ / _____
                                    Month   Year

Today I feel

Happy

Okay

Surprised

Calm

Nervous

Sad

Tired

Angry

Today I'm grateful for...

1. _____

2. _____

3. _____

4. Choose your favorite from the list and draw a star ☆ beside it.

Today I'm most grateful because _____ brought me joy.   (someone or something)

What is one other thing that was nice about today? Draw a picture or write about it.

Date: S M T W Th F S _____ /_____
                                    Month   Year

Today I feel

😀 Happy
🙂 Okay
😮 Surprised
😌 Calm
🙁 Nervous
😞 Sad
😫 Tired
😠 Angry
♡

Today I'm grateful for...

1. _____

2. _____

3. _____

4. Choose your favorite from the list and draw a star ⭐ beside it.

One thing about school that I'm most grateful for is _____
_____ .

What brought you joy today? Draw a picture or write about it.

Date: S M T W Th F S _____ / _____
                                    Month   Year

Today I feel

| Happy |
| Okay |
| Surprised |
| Calm |
| Nervous |
| Sad |
| Tired |
| Angry |

Today I'm grateful for...

1. _____

2. _____

3. _____

4. Choose your favorite from the list and draw a star ☆ beside it.

Today I'm most grateful because _____ brought me joy.
                                    (someone or something)

What is one other thing that was nice about today? Draw a picture or write about it.

Date: S   M   T   W   Th   F   S   _____ / _____
                                          Month   Year

Today I feel

Happy

Okay

Surprised

Calm

Nervous

Sad

Tired

Angry

Today I'm grateful for...

1. _____

2. _____

3. _____

4. Choose your favorite from the list and draw a star ☆ beside it.

Today I'm most grateful because _____ brought
me joy.   (someone or something)

What is one other thing that was nice about today? Draw a
picture or write about it.

Date: S   M   T   W   Th   F   S   _____ / _____
                                        Month   Year

Today I feel

Happy

Okay

Surprised

Calm

Nervous

Sad

Tired

Angry

Today I'm grateful for...

1. _____

2. _____

3. _____

4. Choose your favorite from the list and draw a star ☆ beside it.

Today I'm most grateful because _____ brought
me joy.   (someone or something)

What is one other thing that was nice about today? Draw a
picture or write about it.

Date: S   M   T   W   Th   F   S   _____ / _____
                                              Month   Year

Today I feel

Happy

Okay

Surprised

Calm

Nervous

Sad

Tired

Angry

Today I'm grateful for...

1. _____

2. _____

3. _____

4. Choose your favorite from the list and draw a star ☆ beside it.

I am very thankful for my home. The thing that brings me the most joy about my home is _____ .

Draw a picture or write about something that happened at your home that you are grateful for.

Date: S M T W Th F S _____ /_____
                                Month   Year

Today I feel

- Happy
- Okay
- Surprised
- Calm
- Nervous
- Sad
- Tired
- Angry

Today I'm grateful for...

1. _____

2. _____

3. _____

4. Choose your favorite from the list and draw a star ☆ beside it.

Today I'm most grateful because _____ brought me joy.
                                    (someone or something)

What is one other thing that was nice about today? Draw a picture or write about it.

Date: S M T W Th F S _____ / _____
                                    Month   Year

Today I feel

- Happy
- Okay
- Surprised
- Calm
- Nervous
- Sad
- Tired
- Angry

Today I'm grateful for...

1. _____

2. _____

3. _____

4. Choose your favorite from the list and draw a star ☆ beside it.

Today I'm most grateful because _____ brought
me joy.   (someone or something)

What is one other thing that was nice about today? Draw a
picture or write about it.

Date: S   M   T   W   Th   F   S   _____ / _____

Month   Year

Today I feel

Happy

Okay

Surprised

Calm

Nervous

Sad

Tired

Angry

Today I'm grateful for...

1. _____

2. _____

3. _____

4. Choose your favorite from the list and draw a star ☆ beside it.

Today I'm most grateful because _____ brought me joy.

(someone or something)

What is one other thing that was nice about today? Draw a picture or write about it.

Date: S M T W Th F S _____/_____
Month   Year

Today I feel

Happy

Okay

Surprised

Calm

Nervous

Sad

Tired

Angry

Today I'm grateful for...

1. _____

2. _____

3. _____

4. Choose your favorite from the list and draw a star ☆ beside it.

Our bodies are totally awesome! Write one thing about your body that you are grateful for. One thing about my body that I'm grateful for is _____.

Draw a picture or write about things to do (like taking good care of it) to show that you are grateful for your body.

Date: S   M   T   W   Th   F   S   _____ / _____

Month   Year

Today I feel

Happy

Okay

Surprised

Calm

Nervous

Sad

Tired

Angry

Today I'm grateful for...

1. _____

2. _____

3. _____

4. Choose your favorite from the list and draw a star ☆ beside it.

Today I'm most grateful because _____ brought me joy.   (someone or something)

What is one other thing that was nice about today? Draw a picture or write about it.

Date: S   M   T   W   Th   F   S   _____ / _____
                                          Month   Year

Today I feel

Happy
Okay
Surprised
Calm
Nervous
Sad
Tired
Angry

Today I'm grateful for...

1. _____

2. _____

3. _____

4. Choose your favorite from the list and draw a star ☆ beside it.

Today I'm most grateful because _____ brought
me joy.   (someone or something)

What is one other thing that was nice about today? Draw a
picture or write about it.

Date: S   M   T   W   Th   F   S   _____ / _____

Month   Year

Today I feel

- Happy
- Okay
- Surprised
- Calm
- Nervous
- Sad
- Tired
- Angry

Today I'm grateful for...

1. _____

2. _____

3. _____

4. Choose your favorite from the list and draw a star ☆ beside it.

Today I'm most grateful because _____ brought me joy.

(someone or something)

What is one other thing that was nice about today? Draw a picture or write about it.

Date: S   M   T   W   Th   F   S   _____ / _____
                                          Month   Year

Today I feel

😀 Happy
🙂 Okay
😮 Surprised
😌 Calm
😟 Nervous
😢 Sad
😫 Tired
😠 Angry
♡

Today I'm grateful for...

1. _____

2. _____

3. _____

4. Choose your favorite from the list and draw a star ☆ beside it.

A birthday is a very special day! What is one thing about your last birthday that you are grateful for? One thing that I'm grateful for about my last birthday is _____

_____ .

Write a note or draw a picture to let someone know how they brought you joy on a birthday.

Dear _____ ,

When you _____ it brought me joy on my birthday.

Thank you,

_____

Date: S M T W Th F S _____ / _____

Month   Year

Today I feel

Happy

Okay

Surprised

Calm

Nervous

Sad

Tired

Angry

Today I'm grateful for...

1. _____

2. _____

3. _____

4. Choose your favorite from the list and draw a star ☆ beside it.

Today I'm most grateful because _____ brought
me joy.   (someone or something)

What is one other thing that was nice about today? Draw a
picture or write about it.

Date: S   M   T   W   Th   F   S   _____ / _____
                                        Month   Year

Today I feel

😀 Happy
🙂 Okay
😮 Surprised
😌 Calm
😟 Nervous
😞 Sad
😓 Tired
😠 Angry
♡

Today I'm grateful for...

1. _____

2. _____

3. _____

4. Choose your favorite from the list and draw a star ☆ beside it.

Today I'm most grateful because _____ brought
me joy.   (someone or something)

What is one other thing that was nice about today? Draw a
picture or write about it.

Date: S M T W Th F S _____ / _____
                                Month   Year

Today I feel

Happy

Okay

Surprised

Calm

Nervous

Sad

Tired

Angry

Today I'm grateful for...

1. _____

2. _____

3. _____

4. Choose your favorite from the list and draw a star ☆ beside it.

Today I'm most grateful because _____ brought me joy.
                                        (someone or something)

What is one other thing that was nice about today? Draw a picture or write about it.

Date: S M T W Th F S _____ / _____
                                    Month   Year

Today I feel

Happy

Okay

Surprised

Calm

Nervous

Sad

Tired

Angry

Today I'm grateful for...

1. _____

2. _____

3. _____

4. Choose your favorite from the list and draw a star ☆ beside it.

My favorite season of the year is _____.

I'm grateful for it because _____

_____.

Draw a picture or write about one special thing in your favorite season that brings you joy.

Date: S   M   T   W   Th   F   S   _____ / _____

Month   Year

Today I feel

😀 Happy
🙂 Okay
😮 Surprised
😌 Calm
😟 Nervous
😞 Sad
😫 Tired
😠 Angry
♡

Today I'm grateful for...

1. _____

2. _____

3. _____

4. Choose your favorite from the list and draw a star ☆ beside it.

Today I'm most grateful because _____ brought
me joy.   (someone or something)

What is one other thing that was nice about today? Draw a
picture or write about it.

Date: S   M   T   W   Th   F   S   _____/_____
                                          Month   Year

Today I feel

- Happy
- Okay
- Surprised
- Calm
- Nervous
- Sad
- Tired
- Angry

Today I'm grateful for...

1. _____

2. _____

3. _____

4. Choose your favorite from the list and draw a star ☆ beside it.

Today I'm most grateful because _____ brought me joy.   (someone or something)

What is one other thing that was nice about today? Draw a picture or write about it.

Date: S M T W Th F S _____ / _____
Month   Year

Today I feel

Happy

Okay

Surprised

Calm

Nervous

Sad

Tired

Angry

Today I'm grateful for...

1. _____

2. _____

3. _____

4. Choose your favorite from the list and draw a star ☆ beside it.

Today I'm most grateful because _____ brought me joy.
(someone or something)

What is one other thing that was nice about today? Draw a picture or write about it.

Date: S   M   T   W   Th   F   S   _____ / _____
                                          Month   Year

Today I feel

Happy
Okay
Surprised
Calm
Nervous
Sad
Tired
Angry

Today I'm grateful for...

1. _____

2. _____

3. _____

4. Choose your favorite from the list and draw a star ⭐ beside it.

_____ is my favorite music artist.

Their music brings me joy because _____

_____.

Think about your favorite of their songs. Draw a picture or write about why you are grateful for the song.

Date: S M T W Th F S _____ / _____
Month   Year

Today I feel

Happy

Okay

Surprised

Calm

Nervous

Sad

Tired

Angry

Today I'm grateful for...

1. _____

2. _____

3. _____

4. Choose your favorite from the list and draw a star ☆ beside it.

Today I'm most grateful because _____ brought
me joy.   (someone or something)

What is one other thing that was nice about today? Draw a
picture or write about it.

Date: S M T W Th F S _____ / _____
                                    Month   Year

Today I feel

- Happy
- Okay
- Surprised
- Calm
- Nervous
- Sad
- Tired
- Angry

Today I'm grateful for...

1. _____

2. _____

3. _____

4. Choose your favorite from the list and draw a star ☆ beside it.

Today I'm most grateful because _____ brought
me joy.   (someone or something)

What is one other thing that was nice about today? Draw a
picture or write about it.

Date: S   M   T   W   Th   F   S   _____ / _____
                                                    Month   Year

Today I feel

- Happy
- Okay
- Surprised
- Calm
- Nervous
- Sad
- Tired
- Angry

Today I'm grateful for...

1. _____

2. _____

3. _____

4. Choose your favorite from the list and draw a star ☆ beside it.

Today I'm most grateful because _____ brought me joy.
                                              (someone or something)

What is one other thing that was nice about today? Draw a picture or write about it.

Date: S   M   T   W   Th   F   S   _____ / _____
                                          Month   Year

Today I feel

- Happy
- Okay
- Surprised
- Calm
- Nervous
- Sad
- Tired
- Angry

♡

Today I'm grateful for...

1. _____

2. _____

3. _____

4. Choose your favorite from the list and draw a star ☆ beside it.

What is your favorite sports team?_____.
                                      (team name)

The team brings you joy because_____
_____.

Draw a picture or write about things about the team or a member of the team that you are grateful for.

Date: S   M   T   W   Th   F   S   _____ / _____
                                          Month   Year

Today I feel

😁	Happy
🙂	Okay
😮	Surprised
😌	Calm
😟	Nervous
😢	Sad
😩	Tired
😠	Angry
♡	

Today I'm grateful for...

1. _____

2. _____

3. _____

4. Choose your favorite from the list and draw a star ☆ beside it.

Today I'm most grateful because _____ brought me joy.
                                        (someone or something)

What is one other thing that was nice about today? Draw a picture or write about it.

Date: S M T W Th F S _____ / _____
                                    Month   Year

Today I feel

😄 Happy
🙂 Okay
😮 Surprised
😌 Calm
😟 Nervous
😞 Sad
😓 Tired
😠 Angry
♡

Today I'm grateful for...

1. _____

2. _____

3. _____

4. Choose your favorite from the list and draw a star ☆ beside it.

Today I'm most grateful because _____ brought
me joy.   (someone or something)

What is one other thing that was nice about today? Draw a
picture or write about it.

Date: S   M   T   W   Th   F   S   _____ / _____

Month   Year

Today I feel

- Happy
- Okay
- Surprised
- Calm
- Nervous
- Sad
- Tired
- Angry

Today I'm grateful for...

1. _____

2. _____

3. _____

4. Choose your favorite from the list and draw a star ☆ beside it.

Today I'm most grateful because _____ brought me joy.

(someone or something)

What is one other thing that was nice about today? Draw a picture or write about it.

Date: S   M   T   W   Th   F   S   _____/_____
                                    Month   Year

Today I feel

Happy

Okay

Surprised

Calm

Nervous

Sad

Tired

Angry

♡

Today I'm grateful for...

1. _____

2. _____

3. _____

4. Choose your favorite from the list and draw a star ☆ beside it.

My favorite month of the year is _____.

It brings me joy because_____

_____.

Draw a picture or write about someone that you get to spend time with during your favorite month that you are grateful for.

Date: S M T W Th F S _____ / _____

Month / Year

Today I feel

- 😀 Happy
- 🙂 Okay
- 😮 Surprised
- 😌 Calm
- 😟 Nervous
- 😢 Sad
- 😫 Tired
- 😠 Angry
- ♡

Today I'm grateful for...

1. _____

2. _____

3. _____

4. Choose your favorite from the list and draw a star ☆ beside it.

Today I'm most grateful because _____ brought me joy.

(someone or something)

What is one other thing that was nice about today? Draw a picture or write about it.

Date: S M T W Th F S _____ / _____
                                    Month   Year

Today I feel

- Happy
- Okay
- Surprised
- Calm
- Nervous
- Sad
- Tired
- Angry

Today I'm grateful for...

1. _____

2. _____

3. _____

4. Choose your favorite from the list and draw a star ☆ beside it.

Today I'm most grateful because _____ brought
me joy.   (someone or something)

What is one other thing that was nice about today? Draw a
picture or write about it.

Date: S   M   T   W   Th   F   S   _____ / _____

Month   Year

Today I feel

- Happy
- Okay
- Surprised
- Calm
- Nervous
- Sad
- Tired
- Angry

Today I'm grateful for...

1. _____

2. _____

3. _____

4. Choose your favorite from the list and draw a star ☆ beside it.

Today I'm most grateful because _____ brought me joy.

(someone or something)

What is one other thing that was nice about today? Draw a picture or write about it.

Date: S   M   T   W   Th   F   S   _____ / _____
                                          Month   Year

Today I feel

Happy	
Okay	
Surprised	
Calm	
Nervous	
Sad	
Tired	
Angry	

Today I'm grateful for...

1. _____

2. _____

3. _____

4. Choose your favorite from the list and draw a star ☆ beside it.

_____ is my favorite teacher.
        (name)

I'm very grateful for them because _____

_____ .

Draw a picture or write about a day when your favorite teacher did something special for you or your classmates.

Date: S   M   T   W   Th   F   S   _____ / _____
                                              Month   Year

Today I feel

Happy

Okay

Surprised

Calm

Nervous

Sad

Tired

Angry

Today I'm grateful for...

1. _____

2. _____

3. _____

4. Choose your favorite from the list and draw a star ☆ beside it.

Today I'm most grateful because _____ brought
me joy.   (someone or something)

What is one other thing that was nice about today? Draw a
picture or write about it.

Date: S   M   T   W   Th   F   S   _____ / _____
                                              Month   Year

Today I feel

Happy

Okay

Surprised

Calm

Nervous

Sad

Tired

Angry

Today I'm grateful for...

1. _____

2. _____

3. _____

4. Choose your favorite from the list and draw a star ☆ beside it.

Today I'm most grateful because _____ brought
me joy.   (someone or something)

What is one other thing that was nice about today? Draw a
picture or write about it.

Date: S   M   T   W   Th   F   S _____ / _____
                                              Month   Year

Today I feel

Happy

Okay

Surprised

Calm

Nervous

Sad

Tired

Angry

Today I'm grateful for...

1. _____

2. _____

3. _____

4. Choose your favorite from the list and draw a star ☆ beside it.

The best trip that I've ever been on was to _____.
                                                          (place)

It brought me joy because _____

_____.

Write a thank you note to the person who made your best trip possible. Let them know why you are grateful for the awesome trip.

Dear _____ ,

Thank you for my trip to _____.

I am very grateful for the trip because_____

_____

_____

_____.

Sincerely,

_____

Date: S M T W Th F S _____ / _____
Month   Year

Today I feel

Happy

Okay

Surprised

Calm

Nervous

Sad

Tired

Angry

Today I'm grateful for...

1. _____

2. _____

3. _____

4. Choose your favorite from the list and draw a star ☆ beside it.

Today I'm most grateful because _____ brought
me joy.   (someone or something)

What is one other thing that was nice about today? Draw a
picture or write about it.

Date: S   M   T   W   Th   F   S   _____ / _____

Month   Year

Today I feel

Happy

Okay

Surprised

Calm

Nervous

Sad

Tired

Angry

Today I'm grateful for...

1. _____

2. _____

3. _____

4. Choose your favorite from the list and draw a star ☆ beside it.

Today I'm most grateful because _____ brought me joy.

(someone or something)

What is one other thing that was nice about today? Draw a picture or write about it.

Date: S M T W Th F S _____/_____
                                   Month   Year

Today I feel

- Happy
- Okay
- Surprised
- Calm
- Nervous
- Sad
- Tired
- Angry

Today I'm grateful for...

1. _____

2. _____

3. _____

4. Choose your favorite from the list and draw a star ☆ beside it.

Today I'm most grateful because _____ brought
me joy.   (someone or something)

What is one other thing that was nice about today? Draw a
picture or write about it.

Date: S   M   T   W   Th   F   S   _____ / _____
Month   Year

Today I feel

- Happy
- Okay
- Surprised
- Calm
- Nervous
- Sad
- Tired
- Angry

Today I'm grateful for...

1. _____

2. _____

3. _____

4. Choose your favorite from the list and draw a star ☆ beside it.

My favorite holiday is _____.

It brings me joy because _____

_____.

Draw a picture or write about one special thing that happened on your favorite holiday that you are grateful for.

Date: S   M   T   W   Th   F   S   _____/_____
                                              Month   Year

Today I feel

- Happy
- Okay
- Surprised
- Calm
- Nervous
- Sad
- Tired
- Angry

Today I'm grateful for...

1. _____

2. _____

3. _____

4. Choose your favorite from the list and draw a star ☆ beside it.

Today I'm most grateful because _____ brought me joy.   (someone or something)

What is one other thing that was nice about today? Draw a picture or write about it.

Date: S M T W Th F S _____ / _____

Month   Year

Today I feel

Happy

Okay

Surprised

Calm

Nervous

Sad

Tired

Angry

Today I'm grateful for...

1. _____

2. _____

3. _____

4. Choose your favorite from the list and draw a star ☆ beside it.

Today I'm most grateful because _____ brought
me joy.   (someone or something)

What is one other thing that was nice about today? Draw a
picture or write about it.

Date: S   M   T   W   Th   F   S   _____ / _____
                                        Month   Year

Today I feel

- Happy
- Okay
- Surprised
- Calm
- Nervous
- Sad
- Tired
- Angry

Today I'm grateful for...

1. _____

2. _____

3. _____

4. Choose your favorite from the list and draw a star ☆ beside it.

Today I'm most grateful because _____ brought
me joy.   (someone or something)

What is one other thing that was nice about today? Draw a
picture or write about it.

Date: S M T W Th F S _____ / _____

Month   Year

Today I feel

Happy

Okay

Surprised

Calm

Nervous

Sad

Tired

Angry

Today I'm grateful for...

1. _____

2. _____

3. _____

4. Choose your favorite from the list and draw a star ☆ beside it.

Animals can make us smile and bring us joy!

Write what your favorite animal is here. _____

Draw a picture or write about how your favorite animal brings you joy.

Date: S   M   T   W   Th   F   S   _____ / _____
                                        Month   Year

Today I feel

😃 Happy
🙂 Okay
😮 Surprised
😌 Calm
😟 Nervous
😞 Sad
😫 Tired
😠 Angry
♡

Today I'm grateful for...

1. _____

2. _____

3. _____

4. Choose your favorite from the list and draw a star ☆ beside it.

Today I'm most grateful because _____ brought
me joy.   (someone or something)

What is one other thing that was nice about today? Draw a
picture or write about it.

Date: S   M   T   W   Th   F   S   _____ / _____
Month   Year

Today I feel

Happy

Okay

Surprised

Calm

Nervous

Sad

Tired

Angry

Today I'm grateful for...

1. _____

2. _____

3. _____

4. Choose your favorite from the list and draw a star ☆ beside it.

Today I'm most grateful because _____ brought
me joy.   (someone or something)

What is one other thing that was nice about today? Draw a
picture or write about it.

Date: S   M   T   W   Th   F   S   _____ / _____
                                          Month   Year

Today I feel

Happy

Okay

Surprised

Calm

Nervous

Sad

Tired

Angry

Today I'm grateful for...

1. _____

2. _____

3. _____

4. Choose your favorite from the list and draw a star ☆ beside it.

Today I'm most grateful because _____ brought me joy.   (someone or something)

What is one other thing that was nice about today? Draw a picture or write about it.

Date: S   M   T   W   Th   F   S   _____ / _____

Month   Year

Today I feel

Happy
Okay
Surprised
Calm
Nervous
Sad
Tired
Angry

Today I'm grateful for...

1. _____

2. _____

3. _____

4. Choose your favorite from the list and draw a star ☆ beside it.

Write what your favorite toy is here. _____

It brings you joy because_____

_____.

Draw a picture or write about something that you do to show that you are grateful for your toys.

Date: S   M   T   W   Th   F   S   _____ / _____
                                          Month   Year

Today I feel

Happy
Okay
Surprised
Calm
Nervous
Sad
Tired
Angry

Today I'm grateful for...

1. _____

2. _____

3. _____

4. Choose your favorite from the list and draw a star ⭐ beside it.

Today I'm most grateful because _____ brought
me joy.   (someone or something)

What is one other thing that was nice about today? Draw a
picture or write about it.

Date: S   M   T   W   Th   F   S   _____ / _____
                                        Month   Year

Today I feel

Happy

Okay

Surprised

Calm

Nervous

Sad

Tired

Angry

Today I'm grateful for...

1. _____

2. _____

3. _____

4. Choose your favorite from the list and draw a star ☆ beside it.

Today I'm most grateful because _____ brought me joy.
                                        (someone or something)

What is one other thing that was nice about today? Draw a picture or write about it.

Date: S M T W Th F S _____ / _____
                                    Month   Year

Go back through your pages and review the items that you drew stars beside. Choose the 10 that mean the most to you and write them below. Congratulations! You have just created your "Top Ten" list! You can cut the list out and keep it near to help remind you of some of the most important things that you are grateful for every day.

Today I feel

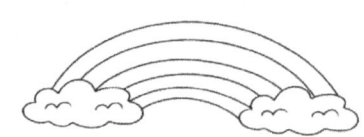

My Top Ten

1. _____

2. _____

3. _____

4. _____

5. _____

6. _____

7. _____

8. _____

9. _____

10. _____

Thank you for purchasing the **What's Good Gratitude Journal for Kids**. We are very grateful! If your kids enjoyed this journal, please leave us a review.

Leaving a review is easy, just follow the steps below.

1. Go to the book detail page.
2. Click on write a customer review in the Customer Reviews section near the bottom of the page.

Review this product

Share your thoughts with other customers

Write a customer review

3. Select a Star Rating.
4. Add text, photos, or videos and click Submit.